flower magic

This edition first published in 2025 by Red Wheel, an imprint of
Red Wheel/Weiser, LLC
With offices at:
65 Parker Street, Suite 7
Newburyport, MA 01950
www.redwheelweiser.com

All rights reserved. No part of this publication may be reproduced or transmitted in any form or by any means, electronic or mechanical, including photocopying, recording, or by any information storage and retrieval system, without permission in writing from Red Wheel/Weiser, LLC. Reviewers may quote brief passages.

ISBN 978-1-59003-573-3

Printed in China

Publisher
Balthazar Pagani

Graphic design and layout
Bebung

Originally published

Vivida

Vivida® is a registered trademark property of White Star s.r.l.
www.vividabooks.com

© 2024 White Star s.r.l.
Piazzale Luigi Cadorna, 6
20123 Milano, Italia
www.whitestar.it

Translation: Pangea – Editing: Phillip Gaskill

Anastasia Mostacci

flower magic

The Secret Language of Flowers

ILLUSTRATIONS BY
Giada Ungredda

Red Wheel

contents

7 — IN THE MAGIC OF THE FLOWER
9 — AS LIFE BLOSSOMS

13
garden of the psychic

flowers that influence the psyche and dreams, facilitating shamanic journeys and connections with the spirit worlds

14 MORNING GLORY
16 PASSION FLOWER
18 BLUE LOTUS
20 POPPY
22 BOBINSANA
24 JASMINE
26 ELDERBERRY
28 HONEYSUCKLE
30 WISTERIA
32 IRIS

34 *bouquets from the garden of the psychic*

37
garden of the heart

flowers that work on emotional expansion, healing, relationships, and self-love

38 ROSE
40 PEONY
42 HIBISCUS
44 LILY
46 AGAPANTHUS
48 AMARYLLIS
50 HORTENSIA
52 CHRYSANTHEMUM
54 GERANIUM
56 TULIP

58 *bouquets from the garden of the heart*

61
garden of the sun

flowers that ignite the inner sun, fostering personal growth and the evolution of the soul

62 HELICHRYSUM
64 SUNFLOWER
66 ZAGARA
68 MAGNOLIA
70 FRANGIPANI
72 BROOM
74 CARNATION
76 EDELWEISS
78 ST. JOHN'S WORT
80 CORNFLOWER

82 *bouquets from the garden of the sun*

85
garden of the inner child

flowers for new beginnings, offering freshness, blessings, and a connection to the inner child

86	CHAMOMILE
88	CALENDULA
90	DAISY
92	PRIMROSE
94	FORGET-ME-NOT
96	LILY OF THE VALLEY
98	VIOLA
100	AZALEA
102	CROCUS
104	SNOWDROP
106	*bouquets from the garden of the inner child*

109
garden of the wind

flowers that promote clarity, cleansing, purification, and the ability to let go

110	LAVENDER
112	NARCISSUS
114	QUEEN ANNE'S LACE
116	SOWBREAD
118	BUTTERCUP
120	MILK THISTLE
122	ANGELICA
124	ANEMONE
126	HEATHER
128	VERBENA
130	*bouquets from the garden of the wind*

133
garden of the senses

flowers linked with magic that influences the material world: abundance, physical health, aphrodisiacs...

134	CLOVER
136	ORCHID
138	GREATER PERIWINKLE
140	YARROW
142	APPLE BLOSSOM
144	HONESTY
146	BAOBAB
148	ECHINACEA
150	MALLOW
152	MARSHMALLOW
154	*bouquets from the garden of the senses*

In the magic of the flower

There is no doubt: flowers are the most communicative part of the plant. They speak to us through colors, geometries, and their confident opening to the world. They are brave; from the moment they are just a bud, they are not afraid to unveil themselves and fully show their nature. Their magic has always been linked to divination and love—who hasn't plucked the petals of a daisy, pondering "they love me, they love me not"?

The power inherent in plants, our companions since the dawn of time, forms an ancient connection that echoes through our collective consciousness. The language of plants is one that our ancestresses, wisewomen connected with the earth, knew perfectly. It didn't matter if they couldn't read or write; theirs was a knowledge made of tradition and experience. Herbs, flowers, and fruits were woven into the fabric of their daily lives, with a sense of mystery seamlessly blending into their routine existence, often without their conscious awareness. Even now, the straightforward act of brewing a chamomile tea not only allows us to enjoy its benefits but also stirs a sense of enchantment within us. The ritual of sipping a cup of this beverage, carefully prepared before sleeping, reconnects us with our witch, wizard, shaman being. Our magical nature awakens in the presence of plants and flowers; each one has its message for us, whispered through the senses.

Anastasia speaks the language of leaves, petals, and pistils; it's as if each of her creations is an intimate dialogue with nature. She understands the subtle intricacies nestled within the rosebuds, amid the delicate petals of yarrow, and at the heart of the viola. She thought of this book as if it were a walk in a blooming park with its different flower beds: the garden of the wind, of the senses, the psychic one, that of the inner child, and so on. I invite you to allow her to guide you, hand in hand, as you meander through the blooming pages of this book, stirring the enchantment that you're already aware resides deep within your heart.

Cecilia Lattari

As life blossoms

I was fortunate to take my first steps in a garden and to watch it grow and transform as I did too. My grandmother had planted many flowers there, creating harmonious flower beds that conversed with one another, telling stories inaudible but fragrant and colorful, generous as blooming is.

With those delicate and fragrant petals, we girls created potions, food for butterflies and fairies, crowns or jewelry, and decorated huts built close to the trees. Gathering small bouquets to decorate and perfume the house, or to give to adults who welcomed them with a smile, I learned that a flower is a gift and a message; it is a being that offers itself and teaches the language of beauty and harmony. Together with a dear aunt, I learned to recognize and admire them, to collect them, to taste the edible and sweet ones, to dry them to then stuff small scented pillows, or to transform them into oil infusions or tinctures. The garden changed with each season, and I watched it undress and dress up in colors and scents, become populated with insects and tiny creatures that found a home among the flowers and stems. There were majestic trees that cast refreshing shade, those on which to climb to pick and eat apricots; there were bushes, hedges scented with bay and lavender; there were persimmons that fell suddenly and grapes that ripened in the sun. And there were the flowers, which with their different shapes and personalities seemed like fairy creatures from another world. In one instant, they were mere buds; in the next, they unfurled to reveal realms brimming with enchantment, showcasing stunning natural geometries and emitting distinctive fragrances that whispered to my receptive senses in the wonder of childhood.

The garden taught me about life by showing it to me. It imparted to me an understanding of the cyclical nature of the seasons and all living things, revealing that blossoming may appear fleeting, yet there is exquisite beauty in transience. It showed me that if a flower were to never fade, there would be neither fruit nor seed. In this wisdom that nature embodies, the flower represents a moment of unmatched beauty, a spontaneous manifestation of its essence, and the generous act of giving of itself.

The flower that opens and gives itself to the world is pure beauty, pure enchantment from which our senses can receive information, nourish themselves, and transform. This is an invitation to follow suit: to open up, to reveal our true selves, and to offer our unique qualities freely, allowing our souls to flourish without adhering to any particular form or version of ourselves.

The flower moves through life lightly, fleeting yet total; it is never halfway in its being or in its giving. It is magical; it is nature in its highest expression, and for this reason it is often considered a ferryman toward invisible realms, ancient as myth, fairylike and dreamy, spontaneous as childhood, secret and sacred as the soul.

Every flower is a unique expression, yet it expresses its uniqueness in the network of relationships of the plant world, where nothing is ever separate. Beneath the surface, all roots are entwined and interlinked. Every flower exists in relation to the earth, water, sun, and air and with the entire plant kingdom. It appears and disappears, blooms and fades, like a dream, a precious image to be kept within us.

The magic of flowers is everywhere, generous and undeniable, and it reminds us at every moment of the beauty of the world, even when we have forgotten it. Flowers, living entities with which we can forge a connection, inspire us to nurture their splendid attributes within ourselves.

The story of our life on the planet is the story of our relationship with plants. While the first *Homo sapiens* date back to about 200,000 years ago, the first plants appeared about 460 million years ago. It's for this reason that they hold a wealth of knowledge from which we can learn a great deal.

While animal life is dependent on others, the plant kingdom is autonomous and transforms its own life into oxygen, nourishment, medicine, and beauty. Plants have the ability to transform sunlight into food and medicine and are the necessary mediation between us humans and our star, between us and life. They constantly create and transform our environment, make life possible, and circulate it, filling it with beauty.

Firmly anchored in the soil and perpetually conversing with the heavens, they remind us that the various planes of existence are intertwined, and that sensuality and sexuality are inherently natural and pure, giving rise to both creativity and connection. Plants make love continuously, among themselves and with animals, and that is how they bloom, fill the air with scent, bear fruit—that is how gardens and forests are born.

Connecting with flowers is an intrinsic aspect of our human experience, a wisdom woven into our myths and folklore. Although this understanding has somewhat faded with time, we can rekindle it by beginning to see plants as entities that should play a more significant role in our daily lives. Cultivating a sacred and magical relationship with flowers will transform us, help us to bloom. We will enter every garden on tiptoe, observing with respect and letting intuition guide us toward one flower or another. We will let their magic come to us.

Anastasia Mostacci

garden of the psychic

Here the flowers have the strangest shapes, the petals are more evanescent, and among their colors stand out the tones of blue and bright white. They fill the night with intoxicating scents and speak the language of dreams, of visions, of the spirit. They create a bridge with the invisible and with mystery, guiding us toward dimensions of expanded consciousness. Here we enter in silence, with light steps and unwavering trust in what cannot be seen but can be felt. Here we enter with one certainty: that of emerging transformed.

GARDEN OF THE PSYCHIC

morning glory

IPOMOEA

This delicate blue or purple bell opens early in the morning and closes as the day passes. Because of its evanescence, the morning glory is associated with the world of dreams.

Indigenous to tropical climes, the morning glory has naturally proliferated across numerous global locales, ranging from damp woodlands to sandy shores.

According to Chinese tradition, a young man in love with the moon, in order to reach her, transformed himself into this flower that climbs toward the sky twisting around itself. Perpetually intertwined with the mystical and the ethereal, the morning glory is synonymous with the realm of dreams and visions. Not by chance, some populations of Central and South America use its seeds during shamanic rituals and for divination. Regarded as entheogens, these seeds contain an alkaloid known to induce potent hallucinatory experiences.

The morning glory is an ethereal flower, which easily spoils if touched. It dies in the evening and is reborn in the morning, inspiring us with renewal and transformation. It is said to be a valuable ally in freeing ourselves from addictions and self-destructive situations. We can carry it with us as an amulet, or we can fix it on the top of our head while meditating to favor the crown chakra. Placed under the pillow at night, it promotes lucid dreams and astral journeys.

• **THE MAGIC OF THE FLOWER** •

The morning glory's magic consists of freeing us and connecting us to the universe, to the mystery, to the infinite. It is akin to a bluebell, whose chime resonates solely with those brave enough to heed the whispers of their dreams.

GARDEN OF THE PSYCHIC

passion flower

PASSIFLORA INCARNATA

A profoundly mystical flower, selected to represent both passion and suffering, it is regarded as a remedy with the power to ease one's pain.

Native to North and South America, the name was attributed to it around 1610 by Jesuit missionaries who saw in its forms a representation of the Passion of Christ: a crown of thorns, nails, and a hammer in the flower, the tendrils as whips, and the leaves as spears.

The passion flower is a plant that regulates serotonin levels and is therefore known for its calming properties. If placed under the pillow in a dream pillow, it promotes restful sleep and vivid dreams. An oleolite prepared with its flowers can be used to massage temples and the cardiac plexus, bringing relief from worries and what weighs on us. It also aids in the release of harmful emotions and thoughts, helping to heal emotional wounds.

The passion flower enhances psychic abilities, promotes heightened spiritual awareness, enables channeling, and induces states of mystical rapture. We can drink it as a tea, meditate in its presence, or take its floral essence.

• THE MAGIC OF THE FLOWER •

The passion flower's magic consists of elevating us: it lifts our heart from past wounds, our mind from ordinary thought, and our spirit from the immanent.

GARDEN OF THE PSYCHIC

blue lotus

NYMPHAEA CAERULEA

Often used in funeral ceremonies to encourage the soul to find the light again, the blue lotus is a symbol of creation, rebirth, and the life-death-life cycle. It is the flower that can take us traveling between worlds.

Mystical and mysterious, the lotus lives on the threshold of realms between light and darkness, life and death. Its roots sink into the mud and shadow, while its chalice-shaped corolla, reminiscent of the maternal womb, opens brightly in the morning only to close again at sunset in a perpetual cycle of endings and beginnings.

As a dweller of the threshold and rebirth, the lotus has always been used in rituals and shamanic journeys to enter communion with spirit guides, ancestors, and elementals in the astral dimension and beyond. The family it belongs to, the Nymphaeaceae, is ancient and primordial, a vessel of ancestral memories that date back well before the appearance of *Homo sapiens*. It can take us back to the origin by inducing a deep meditative state, promoting clairvoyance and lucid dreams.

Moreover, thanks to the mild presence of alkaloids, as an oneirogenic plant it acts as a guide through dreams and opens us to liminal states of consciousness, making us sensitive to different dimensions of reality. Concurrently it acts as a catalyst in rituals and spells, enhancing their power.

• THE MAGIC OF THE FLOWER •

The blue lotus is a flower to turn to in order to open doors and bless a new path. It uplifts the spirit without denying the part of us that is born from the mud and instead brings it to light and welcomes it with love.

poppy

PAPAVER

The poppy's light petals, colored like butterfly wings, gathered around a center rich in seeds as black as the night, speak to us of a flower tied to the realm of dreams.

While this plant is found across Southern Europe, Asia, and North America, evidence from discoveries in Switzerland indicates that the poppy has been known since the Neolithic period. The Sumerians used it for medicinal and recreational purposes.

There are approximately seventy different varieties; the most renowned among them are the opium poppy and the corn poppy, also known as the common poppy. All parts of these poppies contain alkaloids, with the exception of the seeds, which are safe for consumption.

The poppy is linked to sleep and death; it thrives on battlefields, regenerates soil exploited by crops, is offered as a gift to the deceased, and is connected to Thanatos, the Greek god of death, who is depicted with a crown of poppies on his head. But it is also a flower tied to Morpheus, the Greek god of sleep, from which the name morphine—the substance derived from poppies—originates. Thanks to the state of excitement it generates and the visions it produces, it was believed to be one of the plants used by witches to fly and participate in sabbaths.

We can offer it to ancestors to celebrate them, or inspire dreams and visions by preparing amulets that enclose dried seeds and petals or by burning them on charcoal. The plant can also be used for divination. A folk remedy against insomnia consists of fixing one's gaze on the center of a poppy.

• THE MAGIC OF THE FLOWER •

Showing us the fine line between sleeping and dying, dreaming and forgetting, the poppy calls us to be present.

GARDEN OF THE PSYCHIC

bobinsana

CALLIANDRA ANGUSTIFOLIA

The bobinsana's splendid tufted blooms—white, pink, and red—resemble hearts bursting forth with sparks and emerge on a shrub that flourishes in the jungle, close to streams.

This blossom grows in the Amazon Basin and is rarely found outside the forests. For its ability to promote a connection with nature, it is considered a master plant. However, unlike other plants integral to shamanic traditions that are consumed within a ceremonial framework, bobinsana does not possess psychoactive properties.

It is also known as *La Sirenita* because, intrinsically linked to the element of water, its roots extend to a length seven times that of its stem, plunging into the riverbed in a manner reminiscent of a mermaid's tail. The pink of the flowers evokes the enchanting dolphins of the Amazon River, creatures steeped in legend for their transformative and mystical abilities.

Bobinsana is a key component of the dieta, a time-honored tradition involving deep communion with the spirit of nature. This practice includes ritualistic bathing, ceremonial activities, and the consumption of specific plants, all undertaken in solitude and accompanied by a highly restrictive diet. It is said that after a long diet, a mermaid may come in a dream, bringing the gift of a sensation of infinite love.

Beyond the practice of the dieta, we can take bobinsana as an herbal tea to promote lucid dreams and to open the heart, overcoming sadness and pain.

• THE MAGIC OF THE FLOWER •

An emotional healer and vehicle of expansion, bobinsana is a mermaid that awakens our soul's song.

jasmine

JASMINUM

**With its intoxicatingly sweet fragrance
and starbright white blossoms, jasmine infuses the nighttime air,
aptly earning the moniker "queen of the night."**

Native to China, North America, India, and some areas of the Mediterranean Basin, jasmine expresses its mysterious and mystical nature already in its name, which is of Persian origin and means "gift of God."

It is a flower widely used in temples and monasteries of the Buddhist tradition, precisely for its ability to promote spiritual awakening and bring balance to the mind, body, and spirit. In aromatherapy, its properties are known to alleviate symptoms of stress, anxiety, pessimism, and depression while also promoting improved sleep.

Burned as incense, thanks to its hypnotic aroma, jasmine expands presence and facilitates meditation and the release of traumatic emotions crystallized in the body. Drunk in infusion, it purifies and broadens our perspective, honing our intuition and deepening our spiritual connection.

On nights when the full moon graces the sky, we may draw near to jasmine and entreat it for our heart's desires, placing a coin beside it as an offering, so that our dreams may blossom forth with the same swift abundance as its fragrant blooms. Planted near the house, it attracts joy, abundance, and prosperity.

THE MAGIC OF THE FLOWER

With its heady and enigmatic aroma, jasmine effortlessly instills a sense of calm and mindfulness, leading us toward a state of harmony where all can be achieved with ease, guided by a lucid and assured perception of our desires.

GARDEN OF THE PSYCHIC

elderberry

SAMBUCUS NIGRA

The elderberry's flowers, which look like light and fluffy clouds, and its floral and fruity scent and taste, make us think of the realm of fairies. As soon as we approach, they bring magic into our lives.

Elderberry is an ancient plant, present since the Stone Age. The name derives from the Greek *sambýke*, a stringed musical instrument. Since then, elderberry has remained associated with music. It was used to craft flutes, most notably the enchanted one that features in Mozart's eponymous composition, famed for its spell-protective properties.

It is often referred to as a plant of protection, particularly against negative energies and black magic. It has been utilized in divination and in crafting amulets, and when planted outside homes and stables, it serves as a guardian.

Every part of the elderberry is used for medicinal, culinary, and magical purposes. It is therefore a valuable resource, yet tradition dictates that we should pay homage to its guardian spirit before harvesting any part of it. This involves kneeling before the plant to honor and express gratitude to the dryad known as Hylde Moer, or "Mother Elderberry." It is said that by falling asleep under the flowering plant, we will dream of the world of fairies.

Very dear to pagan traditions for its medicinal, protective, and auspicious properties, it instead assumes a more ambiguous connotation in the Christian tradition, being the tree on which Judas hanged himself.

• **THE MAGIC OF THE FLOWER** •

Elderberry is a guardian of the threshold: it teaches us to hold opposites together and become ourselves, the first instruments of union.

# honeysuckle

LONICERA

**An anthem to life, joy, and serenity,
honeysuckle fills the evening air with its intoxicating scent,
while its sugary nectar attracts butterflies and bees.**

Native to Asia, North America, and Europe, honeysuckle is a vigorous climbing plant that can ascend to heights of up to thirty feet, epitomizing the qualities of generosity and growth.

Since ancient times, honeysuckle has been used to bring joy and economic prosperity and to keep away bad influences. The indigenous peoples of northeastern Argentina traditionally consumed the flowers in autumn and spring to bolster their immune systems in response to the changing seasons. The sweet blooms are indeed edible and cherished by both humans and fairies, in stark contrast to the berries and leaves, which harbor saponins and are poisonous.

Honeysuckle grows and thrives in liminal spaces such as fences and half-shade areas, serving as a botanical beacon to altered states of awareness, such as meditation or hypnagogic and hypnopompic phases. Gently massaging the forehead with fresh flowers can soothe the mind and help us stay in these states more easily, while also promoting prophetic dreams and psychic visions.

• THE MAGIC OF THE FLOWER •

Honeysuckle is a rope to which we can cling, thrown by the Great Mystery to support us in challenging moments and help us rediscover the sweetness of the present. It allows us to travel beyond our limits, embracing new possibilities.

wisteria

WISTERIA

Everything turns into a dream when the sunlight filters through the wisteria's cluster flowers, ranging from soft blue to violet.

Native to China and Japan, wisteria is a plant that can live for a long time and reach up to fifty feet in height, climbing on any support, so much so that it can sometimes be invasive. The sweet scent accompanies the showy bloom, which appears between May and June, before the leaves.

It is believed that Japanese emperors would take bonsai with them on their journeys to distant lands, offering the miniature trees as tokens of goodwill and friendship. In Jodo Shinshu Buddhism, wisteria is a symbol of brightness but also of the continuous transformation of life, serving as an invitation to savor the beauty of the present moment.

The seeds and stems are toxic. The flowers, however, are edible and can be utilized to create delightful fritters or to infuse into a tea. This can aid in expanding our perspective on a given situation, viewing conflicts as chances for personal development, restoring clarity during challenging times, and appreciating the worth of our endeavors. Their scent helps in meditation, channeling, and overcoming the fear of intimacy.

Wisteria is an ally in our psychic development and on the path to wisdom.

• THE MAGIC OF THE FLOWER •

The wisteria's spiral growth reminds us how the evolutionary path proceeds in the same way, with a cyclical course of death and rebirth dotted with explosive moments of fragrant blooming.

GARDEN OF THE PSYCHIC

iris

IRIS

With its flowers of thin, curled petals arranged like a three-dimensional star, the iris seems like a fairy creature or a character from the world of dreams.

There are about three hundred species of the genus *Iris*, and just as the name suggests, they express themselves in all the colors of the rainbow. However, the most iconic irises are undoubtedly those that bloom in the classic shades of blue, purple, and white. Its name indeed comes from that of the Greek goddess Iris, personification of the rainbow, messenger of the gods, and symbol of the connection between heaven and earth. According to certain myths, it was she who devised the Greek alphabet and crafted the earliest written messages, thereby enabling communication between beings from disparate realms. The flower that takes its name from her embodies her energy of communication and connection with the divine, the mystical, and the world of dreams.

In its forms and colors, in its delicacy and evanescence, the iris appears as if conjured from a dream, embodying the essence of imagination and transformation. In light of these virtues, we can turn to it when we want to communicate with the spiritual realms and increase our intuition and psychic abilities. It is a flower that cleanses the space from dense energies, helping us to release emotional blocks and promoting inner peace.

Irises can be offered, burned as incense once dry, simply contemplated, or brought into a space to raise its vibration.

• THE MAGIC OF THE FLOWER •

The iris is a magical bridge made of hope, faith, and inner strength. It knows how to connect us to our dreams, giving us the ability to communicate and pursue them.

Bouquets

FROM THE GARDEN OF THE PSYCHIC

Weaving honeysuckle and elderberry supports us in transiting threshold places and trusting the mystery of life.

We combine jasmine, bobinsana, and poppy to awaken a state of presence and clear vision.

Wisteria and passion flower have a powerful effect in lifting us toward a state of transcendence, while a delightful array of blue blooms—including morning glory, iris, and blue lotus—serve as our guides through the realm of dreams.

garden of the heart

In the Garden of the Heart, the shades of color are infinite, as are the forms of love and the possibilities of our heart to expand to integrate them all. The magic of the flowers in this garden uses the language of emotions, relationships, and self-love to open the way of the heart and guide us toward acceptance, inclusion, and understanding.

The flowers embrace life, drawing sustenance from the air, water, earth, and sun, and in return they offer themselves with boundless generosity and without reservation. In this, even a small flower can be a great teacher.

GARDEN OF THE HEART

rose

ROSA SPP.

Amid the soft petals and the blossoming corolla that unfurls in a gesture of giving lie thorns: sharp spines that serve as a reminder of the necessity to preserve the integrity of our personal boundaries and to temper our openheartedness with judiciousness.

Sacred to Aphrodite, the Greek goddess of beauty and love, the rose has always been associated with meanings of love: unconditional and fiery, sacred and devoted. It stands as a symbol of both union and passion. At the same time, by tying itself to all its manifestations, from the Great Mother to the Madonna, it represents one of the most powerful incarnations of the maternal spirit, from which its teachings and its healing and protective powers derive. It teaches us to honor sensuality as something intrinsically sacred, as an innocent and natural expression of life. As an emblem of Venusian qualities and creative energies, it invites us to see beauty and to enjoy everything.

The rose is a member of the Rosaceae family, encompassing a diverse array of ancient, modern, and botanical varieties, with approximately 250 species found across Europe, North America, Africa, and Asia. Each color carries a different shade of meaning: while the pink rose speaks to us of openness, sweetness, and compassion, the magenta rose is more connected to sexuality, the orange rose to trust in life, and the yellow rose to strength and personal power. The white rose helps us see the obstacles and shadows that separate us from love, while the red rose is an emblem of visceral passion.

• THE MAGIC OF THE FLOWER •

The rose is a flower that opens the portal of the heart, freeing it and cleansing it of remnants of the past, healing wounds, rebuilding a balanced self, and nourishing our self-love so that it is possible to open ourselves to life vibrating in an energy of pure love.

GARDEN OF THE HEART

peony

PAEONIA

The peony blooms once a year and for short periods, but it can do so for one hundred years in a row. Its abundant and generous beauty nourishes the heart without holding back; it teaches us to trust in beauty and the sweetness of waiting.

It is a full and rich flower, the incarnation of Paean, physician to the Greek gods, who cured Hades with the roots of this plant, the only one to be cultivated on Mount Olympus. Widely used in cosmetics, phytotherapy, and Chinese medicine, the peony has a special connection with the moon and helps to balance its influences. It brings equilibrium between yin and yang energies, between male and female polarities, and is therefore a good omen in marriages and unions.

Also called mountain rose, it differs from the rose by the absence of thorns. Its medicine is sweet, nourishing, drains pain, and reconnects with trust, reminding us that beauty will save the world. Its essence vibrates at the frequency of the heart, and its mother tincture is used as a cure for heart problems.

Regarded as a talisman of good fortune, it is crafted into protective amulets and sachets, which are then placed beneath the pillow to fend off nightmares. With the dried petals, one can prepare incenses to invoke healing energies.

• THE MAGIC OF THE FLOWER •

Healing in sweetness, healing in love, evolving in joy and trust. Return to opening ourselves to beauty and inviting it in, year after year, now and forever, because the world needs beauty and the heart needs to love.

GARDEN OF THE HEART

hibiscus

HIBISCUS SABDARIFFA

Its vibrant colors, the delicacy of its petals, and the harmonious beauty it emanates are nourishment for the eye and the heart; the hibiscus is a flower that offers itself, inviting us to suck the nectar of life like hummingbirds.

Belonging to the Malvaceae family and widespread in tropical, subtropical, and warm temperate climates around the world, hibiscus comes in hundreds of different species. A symbol of beauty, femininity, and grace in many different traditions and cultures, it is associated with the heart chakra and therefore with compassion, empathy, and unconditional love.

It is used in weddings and also in ceremonies related to pregnancy and childbirth for its connection with fertility, vitality, and good health. Moreover, it encapsulates the sacred feminine through its attributes of nurturing, intuitive wisdom, and emotional sensitivity.

It has aphrodisiac properties and for this reason is also used in love spells. Its brilliant colors light up every place with magic, making each locale more sacred and alive. Burning the dried flowers as incense can increase passion in the room. Due to its connection with the water element, it is excellent in baths and for preparing an infusion to invigorate and spritz around rooms. Karkadé, a drink made from the infusion of its fleshy calyx, is rich in vitamin C and antioxidants, a precious medicine capable of bringing joy and vitality.

• THE MAGIC OF THE FLOWER •

Hibiscus knows how to reconnect us to spontaneity, to the ease and joy of opening up and blossoming. It invites us to dance through life with lightness and grace, vibrating and offering all our colors.

lily

LILIUM

A flower that evokes purity, innocence, and humility; white as snow, with its persistent and sweet fragrance, the lily speaks to us of immortality, hope, and integrity.

From ancient Egypt to Minoan culture, from Assyria to Jerusalem, this flower has been cultivated for over 4,000 years. It has been an integral part of human history, continually inspiring those who created works of art in its honor and depicted it time and again, celebrating it as a potent symbol. In Greek mythology, it is believed that as Hera breastfed Heracles and bestowed immortality upon him, a few drops of her milk spilled onto the earth, giving rise to the lily, while others arced across the heavens, creating the Milky Way.

Consecrated to the Virgin Mary and associated with many religious figures as an emblem of holiness, the lily is also considered a funerary flower, as it invites the deceased to present themselves pure before the divine.

It is attributed with magical powers of protection against wounds, spells, and nightmares. Used in love potions, especially to inspire devotion, and in beauty rituals, it is a flower connected to Venus, Easter, and the spring equinox, a time when cyclic energies express regeneration, resurrection, and innocence.

• THE MAGIC OF THE FLOWER •

The lily's magic evokes the strength of rebirth. It conveys the potential to reconnect with the innate purity of our hearts, to the ever-renewable innocence within us. It emanates an auroral beauty that we can awaken in ourselves, thanks to its presence, every time our soul needs to renew itself and prepare to bloom once again.

agapanthus

AGAPANTHUS AFRICANUS

The color of this flower has inspired countless artists in their "blue periods." In its most dreamy qualities, the blue of the agapanthus speaks to us of its connection with the sky and the air, awakening mysticism and magic in those who open themselves to receive its precious essence.

Also known as the Lily of the Nile, the agapanthus is a plant native to Southern Africa. Its name, however, dating back to the Victorian era, comes from the Greek and literally means "flower of love"—which unmistakably reflects the bond between this blossom and the purest form of love: unconditional, unmotivated, and infinite.

Agape indeed refers to the dimension of childbirth and motherhood. In South Africa, it is commonly employed in the crafting of amulets for pregnant women, designed to safeguard the well-being of their unborn children. While used in the traditional medicine of the Xhosa people, who also recognize the flower's oneirogenic qualities, it is utilized primarily for its ability to cleanse the channels with the invisible world and facilitate dream communications with one's ancestors.

For this reason, placing the roots or a piece of leaf under the pillow can help one to have vivid and meaningful dreams.

In its forms and color, agapanthus speaks to us of a love that goes beyond romanticism, beyond generations and the veil of the visible. It reminds us that we are not alone but supported and protected by those who love us, transcending both space and time.

• THE MAGIC OF THE FLOWER •

Agapanthus is a ferryman. It enables us to open our hearts more fully, revealing the nurturing tapestry of love that underpins all that we are connected to. Its blue vibration inspires us to transcend our limits.

amaryllis

AMARYLLIS PARADISICOLA

A winter flower as red as a beating heart nestled in the snow, the amaryllis stands as a radiant beacon piercing the gloom. It serves as a poignant reminder that life can thrive even amid the bleakest moments, that hearts can unfurl, and that light can always find its way back to brighten our journey.

Native to South Africa, the flowering of the amaryllis begins in December and continues throughout the winter, expressing strength and majesty.

Its name, which means "splendor and brilliance," comes from that of a young nymph, Amaryllis, who fell in love with Alteo, a shepherd and lover of plants and flowers who would give his heart only to the one who would bring him a flower never seen before. Guided by the counsel of the Oracle of Delphi, Amaryllis pierced her heart with a golden arrow for thirty consecutive nights. On the thirtieth night, she appeared before Alteo and from her bleeding heart was born a wonderful, bright red flower.

In South Africa, it is believed that these flowers bring good luck and prosperity to the family and that planting an amaryllis bulb in the garden propagates wealth and happiness. In some cultures, it is associated with femininity and motherhood, thanks to its power to increase fertility and promote a healthy pregnancy. In antiquity, women wore it as a talisman to protect themselves during childbirth.

• THE MAGIC OF THE FLOWER •

Determination, dedication, and self-will bloom from amaryllis petals and give vitality to the blood, to the deep impulses of the heart, activating in us a spiritual growth and inviting us to cultivate soulful qualities and the inner self. The heart, even if wounded, has never been so alive.

GARDEN OF THE HEART

hortensia

HYDRANGEA MACROPHYLLA

Its connection with water is deep and ancient, and so is its wisdom. Through its color, the hortensia reveals the characteristics of the soil's pH, making the mystery manifest and the invisible visible.

In North America, fossil evidence reveals that hydrangeas were flourishing on earth as far back as seventy million years ago. In Asia, the oldest fossils date back to twenty-five million years ago. In Europe, however, its proliferation took place throughout the eighteenth century as its popularity as an ornamental plant surged. The genus name *hydrangea* comes from the Greek and means "water vessel." Its connection to water concerns both the body of the earth and our own: the Cherokee Indians used it as a remedy for kidney stones.

The hortensia is a teacher of understanding, forgiveness, and honesty of feelings and is suitable to accompany empathetic and sensitive people.

Its medicine has to do with knowing how to give and receive with balance, making our heart a place of even exchange, teaching us a fluid and permeable protection. In folk magic, it is used to defend against negative energies. When planted in a garden, it protects the home, helps to set healthy boundaries in relationships, and, precisely for its ethereal qualities, favors contact with fairies and the Little People.

• THE MAGIC OF THE FLOWER •

When experiences and patterns of cynicism and bitterness have made us hard and inflexible as stone, and our body stiffens, crystallizing emotions, the hortensia helps us to return to flow, to soften, to surrender again to the flow.

GARDEN OF THE HEART

chrysanthemum

CHRYSANTHEMUM

The chrysanthemum is a precious flower that recalls the image of the sun. We can translate its name, of Greek origin, as "golden flourishing," and let its bright rays warm our hearts.

Native to East Asia, it grows easily in Europe, Asia, and Africa. Its meanings and uses change from place to place.

A symbol of beauty and royalty, the chrysanthemum is the national flower of Japan, where it is used a lot in cooking or in infusions, as a curative tea, for its antiseptic properties. In Australia, the flower is a traditional Mother's Day gift, while in Italy, it's associated with the Day of the Dead. Elsewhere, it's presented as a token of good fortune at the start of a new relationship. Let's select it to mark life's milestones, strengthen connections, and commemorate significant occasions.

In Celtic folklore, it is believed that fairies favor the chrysanthemums in gardens as their meeting spots. According to some traditions, these flowers are also crafted into garlands as a means of seeking the gods' forgiveness.

We can use it with an intention of pacifying and protecting our environment and our relationships, or sip its tea when we want to evoke solar qualities in our heart. This act allows us to envelop every aspect of ourselves and others with warmth, much like the chrysanthemum enfolds the multitude of its petals.

• THE MAGIC OF THE FLOWER •

The chrysanthemum's very essence radiates love, awakens within us a profound and lasting sentiment, and nurtures unbreakable bonds. Its magic is connected to life and death and speaks to our heart, which can embrace and celebrate both together.

geranium

PELARGONIUM

Its fresh floral scent, vibrant hues, and effortless charm make the geranium the perfect adornment for gardens and balconies. It's widely believed that these qualities contribute to the geranium's status as one of the most popular flowers. But perhaps it is its essence, connected to the healing of the heart, that makes it so popular.

A humble master, the geranium teaches us to love ourselves, to give ourselves first the love we are looking for outside, cleansing ourselves from judgment, shame, and guilt. It invites us to open ourselves to life and to rise again through forgiveness, first of all of ourselves. It is a flower that nourishes the heart, makes it feel welcome, and protects it from closing due to past sufferings. In the same way, placed at the entrance of houses and gardens, it protects from unwelcome presences while making friends feel welcome and invited.

Introduced to Europe in the late eighteenth century, the geranium originates from South Africa and was already widely used in ancient Egypt for its valuable healing properties, particularly for skin care. Even today it is used in love spells, and it seems that its petals, if burned as incense, can propagate fertility and invite a new soul to incarnate in our life. The petals are also used to prepare amulets with the intent of expanding friendships and a social life.

THE MAGIC OF THE FLOWER

The geranium is the medicine of broken hearts. Its magic guides us through the sufferings of love to discover that when the heart breaks it can become larger, overflow its boundaries, and increase our capacity to love.

tulip

TULIPA SYLVESTRIS

In its myriad of hues, the tulip boasts a distinctive cupped form, beckoning us to envision our hearts as vessels ever open to being replenished.

Native to Turkey, the tulip carries with it the legend of the thwarted love between the stonemason Farhad and the princess Shirin, whose father, in order to separate them, made the man believe that the girl had died. Wracked by pain, Farhad took his own life, only to be followed by Shirin, who did the same upon seeing the lifeless body of her beloved. Tulips were born from the blood of the two lovers, symbolizing the passion that survives death. Sultans used to hang these flowers on their turbans as a protective amulet, so much so that the botanical name *Tulipa* literally means "turban." Popular worldwide since the eighteenth century, they are the national flower of the Netherlands. Every year, as March gives way to April and our gardens burst back to life, the tulip is often among the first to grace us with its vibrant hues, rekindling our sense of hope and love. A tulip bulb can be given as a promise of love or placed on one's own altar—the domestic space dedicated to the sacred—to support one's magnetism and attract a healthy and joyful relationship.

• THE MAGIC OF THE FLOWER •

The tulip's cup shape supports us in having balanced relationships, where there is harmony between giving and receiving. It helps us to rediscover the awareness of the constant flow of love in which we are immersed, allowing us to let go of fear and opening us up to receive what we desire.

Bouquets

FROM THE GARDEN OF THE HEART

Combining rose, hortensia, and agapanthus will open the heart, expanding our limits.

If the heart needs to heal, we choose amaryllis, geranium, and peony.

To bring balance to relationships and the ability to give and receive, we opt for tulip and hibiscus.

When the love we feel is everlasting and goes beyond life itself, we combine lilies and chrysanthemums.

garden of the sun

The sun is our central fire, our star. It is around the sun that our life is oriented and can prosper, and everything is nourished. In this garden, there are flowers that celebrate life, light, and sustenance. The plant kingdom feeds on light and transforms it into nourishment for other beings. The sun bestows its warmth upon us, just as the flowers graciously offer their beauty, their fragrance, and their qualities that ignite in us the magic and ability to do the same: to give of ourselves and shine without shame.

helichrysum

HELICHRYSUM ITALICUM

Helichrysum, with its enduring bloom, epitomizes eternal love, inner fortitude, and self-assurance. It conveys a message of resilience and perseverance amid life's enigmatic challenges and hurdles.

For its brightness, golden flower heads, and unmistakable scent, helichrysum, capable of activating the inner sun and the golden qualities of our soul, can be considered the flower of *kintsugi*—the Japanese art of repairing broken objects with gold, transforming the cracks into places of great beauty. Much like an eternal sun, this resilient flower radiates warmth and casts light upon our scars, beckoning us to acknowledge and infuse them with gold. In doing so, we may mend and transmute our volatile emotional inferno into a wellspring of nurturing and progressive illumination.

Widespread in Europe and the Mediterranean, the magical properties of this flower have been known since ancient times. It was used to adorn the statues of gods, to purify the rooms of the sick, to ward off the evil eye, and to refine intuition and prediction in rituals. It is also a central flower in the Sardinian popular magical tradition, where it was believed that a bunch of it, left to dry for a year and then burned in the bonfire of Saint John, would lead to meeting a loved one and propagate a fruitful and lasting union.

• THE MAGIC OF THE FLOWER •

The magic of this small and simple blossom is immense: helichrysum heals wounds, repairs damaged tissues, triggers forgiveness, and brings to light what is always alive in us, even when we go through times of change or difficulty, including the unavoidable losses that punctuate our existence. It is a medicine for wounds that do not heal and activates reconciliation and grace in us.

sunflower

HELIANTHUS ANNUUS

The sunflower is the flower of summer, so in love with the sun that it resembles it in appearance and orients itself to follow its journey across the sky from dawn to dusk. It evokes warmth, joy, and positivity.

Native to South and Central America, the first traces of the sunflower plant date back to 4,600 years ago and were found in Mexico. In the 1500s, the Spaniards brought it to Europe and from there it has spread all over the world.

For the Aztecs and Incas, it was a symbol of solar deities. Native Americans recognized its healing, nourishing aspects and also used it as a dye plant to give fabrics orange and yellow shades. In many folklore traditions, it is linked to good omens, luck, and gifts and is associated with the harvest season and the Litha festival, which occurs on the summer solstice.

Mixing its petals in bathwater, wearing a crown or a necklace of flowers, and drinking an infusion: these are all practices that can propagate fertility and give us vitality, joy of living, and abundance. As a flower that draws its life from solar rays, the enchantment it imparts is intertwined with notions of truth, loyalty, and honesty. It teaches us to do things in the light of the sun, to stop hiding and show ourselves for what we are.

• THE MAGIC OF THE FLOWER •

Like the sun, the sunflower guides us toward personal growth by connecting us with the spiritual realms. It aids us on our path of spiritual growth, activating within us an inner sun that will steer and enlighten our awareness.

zagara

CITRUS AURANTIUM

With its fresh fragrance that promises sweet and juicy fruits, zagara expresses spring and heralds the warmth and triumph of the sun.

The word *zagara* is of Arabic origin, signifying "sparkling white" and used to describe the blossom of citrus trees, especially that of the Seville orange. It is the flower of Mediterranean countries, characteristic of southern Italy and especially of Sicily.

It perfumes the spring nights, evoking sweetness and pure joy. A water is extracted from orange blossoms that has multiple uses both in Middle Eastern and Italian pastry. It imparts a distinctive floral essence that perfectly encapsulates the vibrant spirit of spring and the vitality of nature's awakening. It has calming and soothing effects on the skin as well as many other phytotherapeutic benefits.

Zagara's magical uses are connected to solar energy, of which it is a direct emanation. We choose zagara and orange to amplify inner and outer beauty, strengthen marital love, and attract wealth and success.

A bath with orange flowers or directly with the aromatic water can be a true regenerating ritual. Spraying the water in the house or at the workplace brings peace and prosperity, while using it as a tonic on the face will reveal our beauty, enhancing it as if we were constantly illuminated by a ray of spring sunshine.

• THE MAGIC OF THE FLOWER •

Zagara's radiant energy can greatly support the expansive growth of the self, guiding us toward a bright future supported by the benevolent rays of the sun.

magnolia

MAGNOLIA

The magnolia's large and beautiful flowers last a long time and speak to us of the beauty that is maintained and grown over time: the beauty of maturity and the grace of transformation.

Present on earth for twenty million years, the magnolia is native to the Americas, India, and New Guinea. It encompasses roughly eighty species, comprising both trees and shrubs, all distinguished by their profuse and vibrant blossoms. The trees can live for over a century, standing as a testament to endurance and the lasting nature of things, be they relationships, creative endeavors, or professional ventures.

Legend has it that the first magnolia grew on the tomb of Confucius, the Chinese philosopher who promoted an individual and social ethic based on a sense of righteousness and harmony.

They have pungent-tasting edible flowers, with which we can prepare tea, flavor vinegar, or season rice. A ritual bath immersed in its petals can help us cultivate love for ourselves and recognition; the conical fruits can instead be used to consecrate ceremonial waters or, when burned, to attract prosperity, fertility, and resistance in adverse situations. Planting a magnolia in your garden will attract financial growth and abundance.

• THE MAGIC OF THE FLOWER •

Embodying perseverance, this flower teaches us wisdom and spiritual and emotional growth. Just like its intoxicating scent, our uniqueness persists despite the mutations of our spirit.

GARDEN OF THE SUN

frangipani

PLUMERIA ACUTIFOLIA

A flower with an intoxicating and sweet scent, capable of soothing the wounds of the body and soul, frangipani is revered as an emblem of immortality due to its branches' remarkable capacity to rejuvenate and flourish anew, even months after a pruning.

Native to Central America and the Caribbean, by the sixteenth century, frangipani had spread—probably brought by the Spaniards—to most of the tropical or subtropical countries of Asia before eventually making its way to Australia, Indonesia, and Hawaii.

The Aztecs called it *tlâlcacalôxôchit* and revered it as a sacred plant, capable of strengthening the heart and healing wounds. In the Hawaiian Islands, it is considered a symbol of brotherhood and hospitality. Sacred to Krishna and often used for ceremonial arrangements, these trees are commonly found surrounding temples in India, Bali, and various other tropical nations.

Shamans utilize the floral waters as offerings to the gods, for their fragrance serves as an ideal conduit for prayers and expressions of gratitude. Frangipani also has a place in funeral rites: not only does it bless the souls of the deceased, but it reminds the living of their immortal nature through the cyclicity of existence. Ideal also to bless a sacred union and inspire the highest form of love, it has calming properties and strengthens self-esteem, courage, and the harmonization of the self, elevating the spirit and nourishing the soul.

• THE MAGIC OF THE FLOWER •

Instilling light in us, frangipani guides us to pursue spiritual perfection, which is not just an ideal but a constant practice of presence to oneself.

GARDEN OF THE SUN

broom

SPARTIUM JUNCEUM

Given its ability to thrive in harsh environments, broom has come to represent both modesty and humility, as well as vibrancy and magnificence, thanks to the striking yellow hue of its blossoms.

Native to Europe, broom thrives especially in the Mediterranean climates, though it is also present in western Asia. A solar plant that blooms between spring and summer, its simple beauty reveals its humble essence, which in the Middle Ages inspired the king of France, Saint Louis IX, to establish the Order of the Broom. It was also a plant highly appreciated by both the Greeks and Romans for its ability to draw in bees and enhance honey production.

According to the Roman naturalist Pliny the Elder, the ashes of the broom plant were believed to contain gold, a notion likely influenced by its vibrant color. Furthermore, folklore suggests that the pots of gold guarded by leprechauns at the ends of rainbows are concealed beneath these very plants. Therefore, broom is commonly employed as a good luck charm but also as protection, such as by planting it along animal fences, for example. It was also used to make magical brooms for wedding rituals as a symbol of abundance, fertility, and good fortune.

Excellent fuel for bonfires, it is associated with the traditional Beltane fires. It can be burned prior to meditation and divination to create a space conducive to connection and mental clarity.

• THE MAGIC OF THE FLOWER •

Let's search for broom when we need to distill gold and honey, whether through fire and the alchemical process or simply by connecting to the abundance of everything.

carnation

DIANTHUS BARBATUS

A flower symbolic of political movements, revolutions, struggles driven by ideals, and the will to create a better world, the carnation is evocative of virtue and nobility.

Indigenous to the Mediterranean region, there is evidence that the carnation was already in use during ancient Roman times, where it served as a remedy for poisons and the plague. The botanical genus *dianthus* derives from the Greek words *dios*, signifying "god," and *ànthos*, meaning "flower"; therefore, it literally translates to "flower of the gods."

In Christian symbolism, it signifies the embodiment of God, or alternatively the sorrowful tears shed by Mary at the crucifixion of her son. It is also found as a floral motif in mosques and Islamic art.

It is a flower that embodies ardor, that passionate and alive inner fire that, passing through the heart, can express itself in the highest manifestations. It evokes healing, protection, and the joy of living; precisely because of the luminous vibration it emits, it attracts birds, bees, and butterflies. Planting carnations in one's garden is also an invitation for fairies.

It can be placed in protective bags to carry with you, or being edible, it can also be added to food so that it can nourish and strengthen us.

• THE MAGIC OF THE FLOWER •

When our inner spark dims or dwindles, we can reignite it with the enchanting power of the carnation, which aids us in restoring our vigor and zest for life. It knows how to fuel our spiritual fire, help us rediscover passion, and connect us to high ideals.

edelweiss

LEONTOPODIUM ALPINUM

Edelweiss is the symbol of the mountains and the courage to climb a little closer to the sun. Seeing a stretch of it in the high reaches is an unforgettable and exciting spectacle.

The fragile flower edelweiss, meaning "noble white," is distinguished by its petals, which are cloaked in a fine white down that shields it from the sun and the harsh conditions of its habitat. Inextricably linked with the Alps, it actually originated in the Himalayas and Siberia, regions from which it appears to have dispersed during the Ice Age. It can be found at altitudes from 6,500 to 9,800 feet, and its history and popularity are intertwined with the dawn of mountaineering, through which it has become an emblem of courage and nobility of spirit.

    A legend tells of a little star that came down from the sky to keep company with a lonely peak, which, to thank the little star, gave it its woolly veil so that it would not feel cold. Since antiquity, it has been recognized for its magical powers. Besides serving as an antidote for certain poisons, it was believed that burning it as incense would shield livestock from malevolent spirits.

    It represents an invitation to reach often inaccessible places, challenging oneself to climb and evolve, aiming toward the sun.

• THE MAGIC OF THE FLOWER •

Edelweiss speaks to us of the purity of the high mountains and instills in us their qualities. Its essence emanates courage, tenacity, resilience, and eternal youth, inseparably exalted by the breath of the fresh pastures where it grows, shining in the sun. Let's seek it when we need to feel like stardust again.

st. john's wort

HYPERICUM PERFORATUM

Small, golden yellow, and radiant, with a five-pointed corolla, St. John's wort is the symbol of the triumph of the sun. Generously bestowing its light upon all, it warms without scorching, offering healing and nourishment to the soul.

Known and used since ancient times, this flower is the quintessence of solar energy. It blooms around the summer solstice to activate within us the inner sun—a source of wealth, healing, and vitality.

Among its magical powers, from which the nickname "devil's scourge" is derived, it was said to have the ability to ward off evil entities. Nowadays we can harness its properties to send away shadows, fears, and blocks and resolve discordances that hinder our journey toward living authentically and fully realizing our potential and innate talents.

The early Christians nicknamed St. John's wort "St. John's herb" because of the shape of its corolla, which resembles a halo and when picked releases a red liquid, symbolizing the blood shed by the saint. It is no coincidence that St. John's wort water, a time-honored tradition that remains very much alive today, includes this ingredient; it is reputed to bestow protection against spells and illnesses. St. John's wort is also associated with sabbaths and midsummer rites, being one of the magical plants of witches.

Considered a bearer of light, it has antidepressant effects and can help us in times of darkness and difficulty.

• THE MAGIC OF THE FLOWER •

St. John's wort protects us by activating the strength of the sun stored within us. Its magic has to do with radiance: when we shine with our own light, nothing can obscure us.

GARDEN OF THE SUN

cornflower

CENTAUREA CYANUS

The crystalline and shining blue that stands out in the gold of the wheat fields, together with the red of the poppies, has become a rare sight. And it is precisely of vision, of gaze, and of light that this flower speaks.

The cornflower's origins are steeped in antiquity: some 12,000 years ago, it flourished across the British Isles and was even discovered in the tomb of Tutankhamun at Thebes, its hue remarkably preserved. However, the use of pesticides has caused this pure spirit to fade away and rarely be found, as if it wanted to preserve its purity. It shows us that if the environment is no longer suitable for our flowering, we can always leave.

Its name has a dual etymology: *cyanus* comes from the young man loved by the goddess Flora, found dead in a field of cornflowers that then took his name. Meanwhile, the genus *Centaurea* brings us back to the centaur Chiron who, when wounded in the foot by a poisoned arrow, cured himself with the juice of this flower.

Traditionally used for painting and dyeing fabrics, it is recognized and employed as an eye drop: it purifies our vision, allowing us to perceive the world anew and to appreciate the beauty in all things, as well as the virtue of simplicity. Burned as incense or mixed with bathwater, it wards off negative energies and also attracts positive relationships and luck into one's life.

• THE MAGIC OF THE FLOWER •

The cornflower is a vehicle of light, and it brings clarity to our vision. Being an inhabitant of the heavenly places, it knows how to connect us to the central light and direction.

Bouquets

FROM THE GARDEN OF THE SUN

To activate the inner fire, we can combine helichrysum, carnation, and broom.

Cornflowers and edelweiss give clarity and purity to our vision of everything.

A bouquet of frangipani and zagara offers a gift of personal growth and spiritual fulfillment, whereas sunflower, magnolia, and St. John's wort help to summon an inner light that steers us toward spiritual development.

garden of the inner child

A garden at the break of dawn, blanketed in fresh dew, is where a child takes their first tentative steps full of life, enthusiasm, and satisfaction.

Here grow flowers that speak to the heart and know how to heal its wounds, rediscover a lost connection, reestablish trust in life, and bless new beginnings.

chamomile

MATRICARIA CHAMOMILLA

With its scent and aroma that have accompanied us since childhood, chamomile is probably one of the most used flowers for infusions, thanks to its ability to heal and care for us with its sweetness.

The chamomile was known to the ancient Egyptians, who had consecrated it to the sun god Ra. This small and humble plant, with its pungent scent and apple-like aroma, has a long history intertwined with folk legends and traditions. Its name indeed literally means "dwarf apple." In ancient times, people washed or immersed themselves in its infusion to attract luck and love. Even today its healing abilities and insect-repelling properties are exploited.

Its botanical genus *Matricaria* refers to the concept of protection and care that characterizes this flower. Its scent alone takes us back to our childhood, stimulating the spiritual healing of the past. It is a symbol of purity and luck.

Drunk or placed in a dream pillow, it promotes sweet rest and lucid dreams that allow us to access dormant memories. Imbibed as an infusion or smoked, it stimulates creativity and inspiration.

• THE MAGIC OF THE FLOWER •

Chamomile is a mother, a guardian. Seek it when you yearn to recapture the pure joy and innocence of childhood; through it, we can feel cared for, welcomed, and supported. Its loving and playful essence makes us truly feel good.

GARDEN OF THE INNER CHILD

calendula

CALENDULA ARVENSIS

**A little orange sun with a balsamic scent,
the calendula's lively presence brings joy, vitality, and energy
but also nourishment and protection.**

Guardian of innocence and the purity of childhood, calendula is one of the sacred plants of Beltane, a Druid festival linked to the cycle of the seasons and a time when the energies of light and life manifest in their most joyful aspect.

In the Middle Ages, it was called *Solis sponsa* or "bride of the sun," aptly named for its daily dance with the daystar, blossoming open at dawn and folding shut at dusk. It also boasts a profound affinity with the moon, as evidenced by its crescent-shaped seeds, and its monthly reflowering echoes the cadence of the menstrual cycle.

It is a flower of protection, and thus it stands as the skin's greatest ally, providing nourishment and shielding against irritation and inflammation. There are many rituals in which it plays a leading role. Garlands can be hung at the entrance of the house to stop negative energies, it can be scattered under the bed for protection during sleep, its flowers can be looked at to improve eyesight, or it can be carried in a bag as a lucky charm for legal matters.

Due to its beneficial effects on skin and mucous membranes, calendula is widely used in mother tinctures or as an oil infusion.

• THE MAGIC OF THE FLOWER •

The calendula's magic lies in healing wounds related to the violation of boundaries, restoring innocence, and blessing the start of a new creative and fertile path. Let us rely on this blossom to return us to that state of purity of spirit that we can reach after healing.

GARDEN OF THE INNER CHILD

daisy

BELLIS PERENNIS

The daisy, emblematic of innocence, purity, and positivity, stands as a guardian for us all, evoking the delightful essence of a spring meadow, replete with its fragrances and the joy of carefree play.

As the guardian of all that is simple and beautiful, the daisy is often the first flower that many of us encounter, opening the door to a realm of imagination and childhood play beneath the open sky.

According to Celtic lore, daisies represent the souls of children who passed away at or soon after birth, returning in this guise to offer solace to their grieving parents. However, it is to Roman mythology that we owe the genus name for this plant: the nymph Belide was transformed into the small flower *Bellis* by the gods, from whom she had asked for help to escape the unwanted attentions of Vertumnus, the deity of woods and seasons. To this day, the daisy is still linked to the simplest and most tender form of divination that playfully accompanies the first throbs of love: that "he loves me, he loves me not," in which, to discover whether our love is reciprocated or not, we remove one petal after another with fear and hope.

This flower's spiritual and healing properties have been handed down through the centuries. The ancient Romans already knew and appreciated it for its decongestant and anti-inflammatory qualities, for which we continue to use it today. It can be consumed in salads or infused as a tea; it can be used in bathwater to rejuvenate ourselves and as a good luck charm for new beginnings.

• **THE MAGIC OF THE FLOWER** •

The daisy's unassuming charm weaves a spell redolent of childhood, rekindling a realm imbued with the crisp vitality of a new shoot. It can dispel the fear of the future by reminding us to have confidence in ourselves.

GARDEN OF THE INNER CHILD

primrose

PRIMULA

At the beginning of spring, under the first warm rays of the sun, the primroses arrive to announce, like tender and joyful girls, the awakening of all nature.

"She who blooms first": inscribed in its name is the nature of this flower that colors the still bare earth with variegated patches, evoking the spontaneity and freshness of the inner child and eternal youth.

The primrose's ability to open the doors of hidden and fairy realms and show access to true treasures has been handed down in various traditions. In Norse mythology, this flower was sacred to Freya, the goddess of love and fertility. She wielded it to unlock the advent of spring, thus earning it the name *Schlüsselblume*, or "key flower." We find the same concept in the Christian tradition, where primroses become the "keys of St. Peter" to Paradise.

The medieval mystic Hildegard of Bingen advised taking its flowers to ward off melancholy and to carry them on the heart to give light and warmth to the soul.

This flower is not only edible but also boasts analgesic, anti-inflammatory, and antirheumatic benefits when consumed. From a more spiritual point of view, it gives lightness, freedom, and carefreeness, making the spirit younger.

• THE MAGIC OF THE FLOWER •

The guardian flower of the border between different dimensions, the primrose can reveal to us what is usually invisible and awaken us from a long sleep, heal us from disillusionment, and connect us to the source of life.

GARDEN OF THE INNER CHILD

forget-me-not

MYOSOTIS

The delicate sky-blue forget-me-not, although very small, symbolizes something huge: the act of remembering, or "bringing back to the heart."

According to a German legend, the forget-me-not is so called because while God was naming all the plants, a little flower, fearing it had been overlooked, cried out, "Forget me not, O Lord!" To which God responded, "That shall be your name."

The ancients considered it a sacred herb and used it as an eye medicine. The allusion to the eyes can also be found within Christian traditions, where the forget-me-not blossom is linked to the Virgin Mary; representing the color of her irises, the flower symbolizes her fidelity and unconditional love.

To this day, it represents the desire, love, and yearning of each of us toward the infinite and the great mystery of life. It symbolizes all that we must not forget: loved ones, friendships, dear ones who are no longer with us, and also our inner child, with their desires and dreams. Forgetting them equates to relinquishing our potential and our becoming, losing sight of our identity and our boundless beauty.

Consequently, we can utilize this flower to craft a bouquet that pays tribute to the departed, forge a talisman to strengthen bonds, or place it beneath our pillow to induce dreams and evoke memories of something or someone.

• THE MAGIC OF THE FLOWER •

Whoever chooses this flower will never be forgotten and will never forget. They will be present to others and to themselves through the heart, a magical place capable of preserving everything that must not be lost. That is the magic of the forget-me-not.

GARDEN OF THE INNER CHILD

lily of the valley

CONVALLARIA MAJALIS

The unforgettable scent of lily of the valley evokes deep and ancient memories linked to childhood and magical worlds, to the realm of fairies, to the most ethereal dimensions.

This flower's botanical name suggests that it flourishes in moist and shaded spots during May, which is the season for both blossoming and reaping. Of European origin, the lily of the valley is linked to communication between people and between worlds. It is a messenger flower, and it is indeed said that it was the favorite of the god Mercury, who loved its scent and believed it sharpened memory.

It is also known as the "fairy's cup," a name inspired by an old legend that tells of fairies leaving behind their drinking vessels in the meadow after a day filled with celebration. To shield their enigma from inquisitive onlookers, the guardian deity transmuted the cups into the delicate white bells of the lily of the valley.

Being poisonous, and therefore not suitable for ingestion, the flowers were used in medicine exclusively for their digitalis action capable of facilitating cardiotonic and diuretic functions.

Lily of the valley can be safely used in bunches placed in the environment and in one's sacred space to promote peace and tranquility, lighten energies, and favor mental clarity. With flowers and leaves, we can create an amulet that helps us in relationships, mending the emotional scars that cause us to withdraw from those around us. Its scent aids in meditation, elevating the mind and giving it lightness.

• THE MAGIC OF THE FLOWER •

The enchantment of lily of the valley lies in steering us toward rejuvenation, igniting our capacity to recall all that has transpired, including latent memories, and rekindling our passion for life along with the prospect of a radiant, bewitching future.

viola

VIOLA

**With its bright colors and shape,
the viola is a flower that brings joy to everyone,
from children to the most seasoned herbalists.**

Native to Southern Europe, its presence colors the woods at the end of winter. The viola hides in the shadow of the pine and the oak like a childlike spirit that needs to feel protected and supported before showing itself to the world.

According to Greek mythology, it was born from Zeus to console his beloved nymph Io, who had been transformed into a heifer by the jealous Hera.

A symbol of delicacy and the depth of feelings, the viola has a gentle and tender soul, but it can help us find inner strength and free ourselves from crystallized emotions. It is similar to girls and women: it supports them in times of transition and transformation of the body, giving them the spontaneity of inhabiting it. It is a teacher of modesty, creativity, and kindness.

We can meditate in its presence, or burn a little and inhale the smoke to summon a subtle energy and pay homage to the spirits during the late winter's awakening. We can let the flowers macerate in oil for a moon cycle and obtain a beneficial oil that can be applied to the chest area and over the heart and lungs to alleviate melancholy and restore us to a state of unadulterated, rejuvenating happiness.

• THE MAGIC OF THE FLOWER •

It is to the viola that we must turn when we feel hardened by life, rigid and constrained by the walls we have erected around us. It will help us find softness and honor our vulnerability, which is the space where joy can bloom.

azalea

RHODODENDRON

The beauty of its flowers, in multiple shades of white, pink, red, and purple, makes the azalea a symbol of femininity, love, and tenderness.

Native to China and Japan, the azalea is a venerable species, having graced the earth for an astonishing seventy million years. The name comes from the Greek word *azaleos*, meaning "dry," reflecting the plant's remarkable capacity to flourish and bloom in a wide range of conditions, even though it has an innate preference for well-drained soils. It is a very long-lived plant that can thrive for up to a hundred years.

Every spring it fills with flowers, which bring with them the message of nature's rebirth and the hope of a new, fertile beginning.

The azalea speaks to us of maternal love and care; it is a flower that enhances our capacity for both offering and receiving hospitality, thereby strengthening emotional bonds and interpersonal connections. It creates that sense of nest and hearth where each of us can take refuge and recharge before spreading our wings again. By caring for our nostalgia for home and the maternal embrace, the azalea leads us by the hand on a journey of acceptance and healing of our inner child.

Incorporating this plant into our garden will not only benefit our own well-being but that of those around us. Meditating upon the azalea's aromatic essence can ground us, fostering a connection to our roots and bolstering our journey of spiritual growth.

• THE MAGIC OF THE FLOWER •

With the tender yet profound essence of maternal warmth, the azalea beckons us inward, guiding us on a journey to learn how to know and love ourselves.

GARDEN OF THE INNER CHILD

crocus

CROCUS

In the aftermath of the celebrations of Imbolc and Candlemas, with spring ready to return, the crocus sprouts in woods, meadows, and gardens, bringing with it the effervescent energy of new beginnings.

A flower associated with beauty and rebirth, the qualities of the crocus have been sung and appreciated since ancient times. The Egyptians used it to treat eye and menstrual pains and for the funerary art of mummification, while Greek mythology extensively embraced its symbolic significance. The flower indeed referred to the beauty of Aphrodite and the figure of Persephone returning from the realm of Hades. In the *Iliad*, the nuptial bed of Zeus and Hera is described as being strewn with crocus flowers. According to legend, there was a young man named Crocus who fell deeply in love with the nymph Smilace. However, she was the favorite of the god Hermes, who out of jealousy transformed his rival into a flower.

Even today it remains a staple in celebrations of renewal, adding vibrant color and cheer to both altars and homes alike, instilling hope and joy for new beginnings.

It's essential to be able to tell apart the celebrated *Crocus sativus*, which flowers in the autumn and yields saffron from its stigmas, and the *Crocus vernus*, which is toxic and should not be ingested. At the height of their bloom, these flowers can be gathered and dried to craft amulets for both adults and children, serving to bless new ventures and relationships. Owing to its associations with renewal and joy, meditating in the presence of this flower can aid in concentrating on one's aspirations and bringing fresh endeavors to fruition.

• THE MAGIC OF THE FLOWER •

With the promise of spring, the crocus's spirit of contagious and radiant joy guides us confidently toward new beginnings, new ideas, and new adventures, including those of a romantic nature.

GARDEN OF THE INNER CHILD

snowdrop

GALANTHUS NIVALIS

"The fair lady of February" blooms around Candlemas Day. Its immaculate bell emerges from the frozen and hard ground to announce the thaw and awakening of the earth.

Both Greek and Latin were drawn upon for the botanical name of this flower. *Gala* in Greek means "milk," indicating its color, while *anthos* means "flower." The Latin term *nivalis*, on the other hand, means "of snow" and refers to the muffled and magical world in which the snowdrop grows. Its verdant stem perseveres, piercing through the snow-covered earth, and with remarkable strength and determination, it ascends toward the light, ultimately unfurling into a delicate white bloom.

It is for this path of ascent toward the light that the snowdrop was associated in Greek mythology with the myth of Persephone and her cyclic return to earth at the end of the six months spent in the realm of Hades. In other cultures, these flowers are used in purification rituals that mark the end of winter.

There's something truly enchanting about witnessing snowdrops sway in the brisk February breeze, eagerly awaiting the first warm kiss of sunlight, and inhaling their delicate, honeyed fragrance. They remind us of the cycles of nature, and they invite us to welcome the arriving spring with open arms, to cast aside our pain and sorrow, and to place our faith in the promise of a fresh start.

Wearing a snowdrop purifies thoughts, and rubbing it on the forehead relieves the sense of heaviness and headache.

• THE MAGIC OF THE FLOWER •

Let us trust the snowdrop when we feel it is time to thaw our energies and let go of ancient sorrows to look with confidence at new beginnings. We cross the darkness without fear as it does, certain that the sun will return to warm us.

Bouquets

FROM THE GARDEN OF THE INNER CHILD

Calendula, chamomile, snowdrop, and viola can be combined for the healing of the inner child.

A bunch of lilies of the valley and primroses can awaken enchantment within us.

Chamomile, azalea, and forget-me-nots are for those in need of nurturing and maternal love.

To facilitate new beginnings, gather a bunch of crocuses and snowdrops or simple daisies.

garden of the wind

In this garden, there is always a gentle breeze that makes plants and flowers dance. The spirits of the air dwell here, and it is they who move things without being seen. This is the garden to visit when we're searching for change, seeking purification, or undergoing a transformation in our lives. The flowers that grow here bring movement, help us let go of the old, and blow into our sails a wind that pushes us forward toward a future that awaits us.

GARDEN OF THE WIND

lavender

LAVANDULA

Its unmistakable scent crosses space and time, and by cleansing us from the superfluous, lavender brings to the surface the deepest truths of the soul. It stirs within us the capacity to express these truths with a clarity and authenticity that is uniquely our own.

Native to the Mediterranean Basin, lavender imposes itself with its scent as a plant of determination, courage, and the ability to maintain balance even when everything collapses. It is hardly surprising, therefore, that sprigs of lavender were traditionally bestowed upon women in labor to grasp as protective amulets, with the belief that the potent scent would imbue them with strength.

But it is also a symbol of unconditional love and fidelity: legend has it that the goddess Venus enchanted men precisely thanks to its scent. Lavender thus protects couple relationships and, if used as an amulet or rubbed on clothes, is able to generate the magnetic force that attracts love into our lives.

Considering its properties, lavender enhances mental well-being and happiness by boosting serotonin and dopamine levels, thereby aiding in both energy rejuvenation and relaxation. In the spiritual realm, it unlocks the power to turn the impossible into reality, specifically by dispelling negative energies. When burned as incense, it scatters the oppressive and dense atmosphere, both in the environment and within oneself.

• THE MAGIC OF THE FLOWER •

Its name, derived from the Latin *lavare*, carries with it the meaning of cleanliness, freshness, and renewal, thus revealing to us all the magic of the plant. Lavender infuses the strength that allows us to get through the moments when the structures that support us fail; it shows us new directions and illuminates the yearnings and truths of the heart.

narcissus

NARCISSUS

This wonderful flower has unique features and a penetrating scent. As it sways in the breeze, its corolla—be it yellow or white—along with its central trumpet performs what appears to be a mesmerizing dance.

A poisonous plant native to the Middle East and Southern Europe, the narcissus is inextricably linked to the myth of Narcissus, a beautiful and cruel young man who rejected all the people who fell in love with him. The gods therefore condemned him to fall in love with his own reflection in a mirror of water, and he died by falling into it.

This myth has given the plant an ambiguous meaning. On the one hand, it is associated with the concept of excessive self-love and selfishness, yet if we look closer, we can perceive this flower as emblematic of a profound metamorphosis: from so-called narcissism to a death and subsequent rebirth through unity with nature itself. And it was precisely this deeper meaning that the Druids were well aware of, so much so that they associated it with purity and the ability to absorb the negativity of human thoughts.

There is no rebirth without death—that's why the ancient Romans believed that this flower grew in the afterlife, and it has been associated with the festival of Ostara and later with Easter.

It is a flower full of fertile energy. Carried with oneself or contemplated, it inspires peace, calm, and the courage to let our egocentric and limited parts die.

• THE MAGIC OF THE FLOWER •

The narcissus leads us beyond the illusion of separation and disconnection from the whole and helps us to let go of those parts of us that are overly self-centered and closed, offering us a rebirth into true beauty, which is unity.

queen anne's lace

DAUCUS CAROTA

Despite growing on the edges of roads amid the dust of dry and arid paths, Queen Anne's lace resembles a refined lace doily created by the skillful hands of nature.

Common across Europe, Asia, and North Africa, this plant features a consumable taproot and a robust stem that withstands even the fiercest winds. The British queen for which it is named had seventeen pregnancies, but only one child survived early childhood, and even that one failed to reach adulthood. It is no coincidence that this flower not only provides solace and sanctuary in the midst of maternal sorrow but also carries the reputation for its potential to induce miscarriages.

The shape of the flower changes over time; initially, it looks like an umbrella, then it flattens out, resembling a lace doily and characterized by a small central point that is darker, an element that makes it distinguishable from the poisonous hemlock. Later, as the seeds mature, it takes on the closed form of a uterus or a nest: a sanctuary, a refuge, a safe space to process grief and pain.

According to tradition, the seeds of Queen Anne's lace should be collected after the flower has taken on the form of a nest, specifically on the first blustery day after the full moon. Rubbing the flowers between the hands will cause the seeds to fall, and the chaff will be carried away by the wind, taking away negative energies with it. We can also use these seeds to create protection amulets.

• THE MAGIC OF THE FLOWER •

Queen Anne's lace shows us the beauty of every phase of life and helps us face loss and pain by finding refuge in ourselves and in the strength of nature.

sowbread

CYCLAMEN

When we walk in the woods, sowbread blooms announce themselves to our sense of smell with an unparalleled fragrance. Delicate and penetrating, it refreshes us and gives us the energy to continue our journey.

Sowbread grows spontaneously in all Mediterranean countries, but also in Somalia and Iran.

Its botanical name comes from the Greek word *kyklos*, which means "circle," a sacred geometric shape that embodies the cosmos, its natural rhythms, and the cyclical nature of all living things. Sowbread conveys its message through its very form: the spherical tuber nestled beneath the soil, the stem's propensity to curl into a spiral upon fertilization, the corolla's resemblance to a womb, and the leaves that echo the rhythm of a beating heart.

Since ancient times, sowbread was considered a guardian of all that moves cyclically: life itself, fertility, and also fortune. It is a poisonous flower for humans, and for this reason, the ancient Greeks had associated it with Hecate, the powerful lunar goddess of magic and spells. It was used for protection against curses and as a remedy against the bite of venomous snakes. In the Middle Ages, for the same reason, it was believed to be connected to the devil.

It is believed that if positioned where one sleeps, sowbread can fend off nightmares and, more broadly, serve to repel negative individuals and safeguard the heart.

• THE MAGIC OF THE FLOWER •

Sowbread's magic consists of reconnecting us to the cycles inside and outside of us, to the waxing and waning of the moon, to the lengthening and shortening of daylight hours, to change as the key to our being.

GARDEN OF THE WIND

buttercup

RANUNCULUS

Simple and elegant, their botanical name associates buttercups with frogs because of a preference for marshy areas. They grow and spread quickly, and just as quickly convey their message.

Native to Asia and the cold regions of the planet, this genus can be differentiated into more than five hundred species. However, the wild variety, the *auricomus,* is the most renowned, carpeting meadows and pastures with a golden hue.

The story of the buttercup is ancient. Numerous Persian and Turkish myths surround it, and it's well documented as having been employed for divination, to foster spiritual connections, and to acquire wisdom. Dried flowers were used to craft amulets, which were then worn around the neck to encourage mental balance. Additionally, they were gathered into protective clusters and hung outside the home. During the summer solstice celebrations, buttercup wreaths were woven to be worn by cows as a blessing for future milk production. It is also said that Jesus created them, transforming the stars of the sky into flowers as a gift for his mother.

This is a flower tied to the world of fairies, who are said to drink and wash their faces and hands in the dew that collects inside them.

All members of the buttercup family are poisonous and should never be consumed. They must be handled cautiously, as skin contact can lead to irritation and blistering.

• THE MAGIC OF THE FLOWER •

The vibrant, iridescent yellow hue of the buttercup's petals conjures images of gold, symbolizing prosperity and abundance. Therefore, it is an ally in speeding up the realization of our dreams.

GARDEN OF THE WIND

milk thistle

SILYBUM MARIANUM

**With its flowers between purple and fuchsia,
its prickly white-veined leaves, and its thorny and wild appearance,
milk thistle is an emblem of protection.**

Native to the Mediterranean, as early as the first century CE, the milk thistle was recognized for its beneficial properties for both body and mind. It was utilized to cleanse the liver and enhance the production of breast milk, and it was also believed to be effective in alleviating melancholy. In Christian tradition, it is associated with the Virgin Mary, and the white sap that oozes from the plant represents the milk that nourished Jesus.

In the Middle Ages, it was considered a remedy against poisons and bites from rabid dogs and was used in protection rituals against natural calamities. It was sown in cereal fields to drive away evil spirits, and for the same purpose, its seeds were burned or carried in the pocket.

Planted in gardens, it is said to keep away thieves and malefactors. When brewed as a tea, it aids in cleansing both our physical and emotional states; it purifies and promotes the elimination of internal toxins while also supporting the fortification and clarity of our personal boundaries. We can utilize its thorns to craft protective amulets, ignite its seeds to produce purifying incense, or simply take them in our palms, express a wish, then blow them into the wind, entrusting ourselves to the spirits of the air.

• THE MAGIC OF THE FLOWER •

Purification and protection are the qualities of this flower. Milk and thorns are its medicine: it teaches us to clarify what nourishes us and what damages us.

GARDEN OF THE WIND

angelica
ANGELICA ARCHANGELICA

The angelica's large umbrellas that adorn the summer meadows boast delicate blooms and emit a fragrance evocative of licorice and juniper, conjuring a blend of comforting and exotic sensations.

The name immediately tells us this is a divine plant. According to popular tradition, it was the archangel Raphael who bestowed it upon humanity, providing a means to remedy a host of prevalent maladies, upon which it exerts numerous beneficial effects.

Angelica loves the cold, so much so that it even grows in polar regions. For the Sámi culture, it is indeed the most important plant and is used in multiple ways: as food, in shamanic medicine, and in the construction of *fátnu,* wind instruments used in rituals.

It is considered a refuge for fairies and angels and can be used precisely to call them and invoke protection, support, and healing. Great care must be taken to correctly identify it, as it bears a close resemblance to two toxic plants within the same family: hemlock and panacea.

It can be burned as incense to enhance focus and aid meditation and the ability to see into the future. It can also be used to make liqueurs, as medieval monks and mountain people did. It can be dissolved in bathwater, used as food, candied to decorate sweets, or employed to flavor savory dishes, given its affiliation with the celery family.

• THE MAGIC OF THE FLOWER •

Angelica defends and protects us just like an angel would, alleviating all evil, keeping it away from us. It stimulates vitality and internal warmth, resources for self-healing and self-purification.

anemone

ANEMONE

The colorful corollas of anemones, which sway in the breeze of the midseasons, are a reminder of the fleetingness of everything and an invitation to savor every moment.

There are more than a hundred different species of anemone, blooming in the autumn and winter in the underbrush and damp places. Some have grown spontaneously in Europe; others come from South Africa or South America.

The anemone was known at the time of the Egyptians, who arranged it in flower bowls inside the pyramids; the Etruscans, on the other hand, cultivated it around the tombs. A Greek myth tells that the nymph Anemone was loved by two winds: Zephyr, who embodied the gentle breezes of spring, and Boreas, the brisk and chilly northern wind. The two, fighting for her love, unleashed strong storms. To put an end to it, and partly driven by jealousy, the goddess Chloris transformed the nymph into a flower, binding her to the two suitors forever—Zephyr indeed makes the anemones bloom, while Boreas blows away their delicate petals. The myth therefore not only accounts for the anemone's brief lifespan but also its epithet as the "flower of the wind." It was also believed to be a flower dear to fairies, who often chose it as a shelter.

Blowing away the petals of the first anemone we come across and making a wish, carrying a bulb in our bag, planting it in the garden: these are all rituals linked to luck, desire, and harmony.

• THE MAGIC OF THE FLOWER •

The anemone embodies the magic of the breath. It contains life and the invitation to be there and enjoy the present moment without putting it off; every moment is precious.

GARDEN OF THE WIND

heather

CALLUNA

Heather flourishes abundantly on the heath, exhibiting a tenacious resistance to the wind while simultaneously exuding a delicate fragrance that is much adored by bees.

Heather has been known and used since ancient times. We have evidence that 4,000 years ago it was used to make soft-scented mattresses, to weave baskets, and to create blankets and manufacture brooms, as well as for firewood.

Its genus name comes from the Greek and means to purify, beautify, sweep. In fact, it was heather that was employed to cleanse temples, not just sweeping away dust but also banishing negative energies and evil spirits. The Druids, ancient Celtic priests, considered it sacred and magical and believed it had supernatural properties. The twigs were burned to cook the sacred bread used during ceremonies. Given that these plants were also regarded as abodes of fairies and portals to the afterlife, the Celts cautioned against sleeping in their vicinity to prevent being spirited away.

If we want to purify ourselves and clean our environments, we can create a bundle of heather and use it as a broom, or we can burn it as incense. With the flowers, you can also prepare an infusion called "heath tea," which is excellent against coughs and rheumatism, and the famous heather beer.

• THE MAGIC OF THE FLOWER •

The magic of heather lies in nourishing hope and making it a medicine that cures melancholy and loneliness. Hope can then become a wind that blows in our sails so that our dreams can come true.

verbena

VERBENA OFFICINALIS

With its blue or purple flowers, long recognized as a remedy that regulates the physical, emotional, and spiritual plane, verbena guides us in achieving inner balance.

Considered a sacred and magical plant by many ancient peoples who recognized its purifying properties, verbena was believed to be capable of countering evil forces, particularly vampires and witches' spells. It was used by the ancient Egyptians and also by the Greeks and Romans, among whom it was offered to the gods in ceremonies to attract their benevolence and ask for grace and fortune. Also called *Herba veneris*, it was associated with Venus, who was often depicted with a bunch in her hands, and with Apollo, god of music, arts, prophecy, and medicine. Celtic bards wove it into crowns to wear to receive inspiration when composing their songs.

The leaves have often been used to activate oracular abilities or attract protection and peace. A beautiful form of divination, which we can also practice today, consists of writing words on verbena leaves and then, having reached a windy place, letting some be carried away to derive a message from those that remain.

• THE MAGIC OF THE FLOWER •

Verbena is known for its ability to enhance and awaken intuition and inspiration, as well as promote mental clarity and spiritual abilities. It dispels uncertainty and doubt, countering the forces that seek to muddle our thoughts and cause us to lose our sense of clarity and direction.

Bouquets

FROM THE GARDEN OF THE WIND

Anemone and angelica stimulate the breath of life.

To feel part of the cycles and the cosmos, we combine sowbread, Queen Anne's lace, and narcissus.

Buttercup and heather speed up change and instill hope in us.

A bouquet of milk thistle, lavender, and verbena will bring great purification, the necessary precursor for allowing new inspirations to pass through us.

garden of the senses

Flowers and plants speak to our senses through colors, scents, shapes, and tactile sensations. In this garden live flowers that can open the doors of this communication because they are connected to the magic that operates on the material plane. They resonate with our physical well-being and vitality, with our fertility, and evoke a sense of abundance and prosperity. They articulate the rich and nurturing dialect of Mother Earth, constantly reminding us of the love and protection we are graced with each day.

GARDEN OF THE SENSES

clover

TRIFOLIUM PRATENSE

With its pink or white flowers and tripartite leaves, clover colors the meadows and brings joy. When it is a four-leaf clover, it becomes a precious amulet, a guarantee of good luck.

For the Druids, clover was a powerful magical plant linked to the sacred number three: the three realms, the three ages of the moon, the three faces of the goddess. They used it as a talisman and in healing rituals. The Greeks and Romans recognized its medicinal properties and believed that it kept snakes away and cured their bites.

According to Irish legends, the Little People dwell in the great expanses of clover, and those who fall asleep among these flowers might meet leprechauns, fairies, and elves and receive a bit of luck, especially if a four-leaf clover is also present. An undisputed protagonist of St. Patrick's Day, clover is at the center of various rituals aimed at favoring good luck.

It is a simple flower but very nutritious and rich in healing properties. When used as fodder, it increases milk production in cows and promotes the regeneration of soils. The same properties that encourage the production of breast milk in women also detoxify the body and aid in reestablishing hormonal balance, owing to the presence of phytoestrogens.

• THE MAGIC OF THE FLOWER •

This flower reminds us of change and the triple essence of everything. Clover teaches us that in simplicity there is access to the complex, and in the everyday there is access to the magical.

GARDEN OF THE SENSES

orchid

ORCHIDACEAE

Widespread throughout the world, the orchid is recognizable for its characteristic winged structure, which expresses itself in a wonderful multiplicity of shapes and colors.

According to the Greek myth, Orchis, a young and beautiful son of a satyr and a nymph, was condemned to death for trying to seduce a priestess of Dionysus during the Bacchanalia. His father prayed to the gods to spare him, and they transformed Orchis into the orchid, a flower with a delicate appearance whose roots are tied to sexuality and desire.

Traditional lore has long extolled the aphrodisiac and curative properties of these tubers, which have been consumed as remedies for infertility and to either stimulate or suppress sexual desire. According to the ancient Greek physician Dioscorides, consuming the larger tuber would increase the likelihood of a father siring a male child, whereas a mother eating the smaller tuber would promote the birth of a female.

Even today in the East, salep—a flour obtained from the grinding of tubers of various orchids—is used as a restorative aphrodisiac. The tubers can also be used to create love amulets.

These flowers are widely used in the handfasting ceremony, a Celtic wedding ritual that dates back to 700 BCE and has been revived by neo-pagan traditions. Giving an orchid to a loved one sets romantic energies in motion and helps communication.

• THE MAGIC OF THE FLOWER •

The enchantment of the orchid lies in cultivating harmony and peace, nurturing the uninhibited expression of love and sensuality, and sparking the alluring and creative energies that course through us.

GARDEN OF THE SENSES

greater periwinkle

VINCA MAJOR

A flower sacred to the Great Mother, the greater periwinkle's vines and petals of characteristic color unite, forging connections upon the earth and reaching toward the sky.

Native to Europe and the tropics, the greater periwinkle is an invasive plant with healing properties. As it contains alkaloids, it should be used with caution to avoid the risk of an overdose, which could lead to a dangerous drop in blood pressure.

It has historically been associated with the magical powers of witches and also with love and death. In fact, an ancient practice called for periwinkle crowns to be placed on the coffins of children to protect them during their passage and to help parents overcome the pain. Dried leaves and flowers were instead put in mattress stuffing to promote love, passion, and fidelity in couples, and the petals were scattered in front of newlyweds on their wedding day.

In addition to favoring the intertwining of bonds and protecting them, periwinkle is a flower tied to memory. According to an ancient legend, the practice of fixing one's gaze on one of its flowers would induce the resurfacing of lost memories.

Dried leaves can be burned to purify an environment of negative energies, while a garland hung on the door or plants in the garden can safeguard the home and foster harmony.

• THE MAGIC OF THE FLOWER •

This flower can be a great ally for us when we want to remember, strengthen frayed or lost bonds, reinforce existing ones, or favor new ones.

GARDEN OF THE SENSES

yarrow

ACHILLEA MILLEFOLIUM

With its delicate white and pink blossoms, accompanied by petite leaves, the yarrow is an unmistakable fixture in meadows and pastures, where its robust roots delve deep into the rich, dark soil.

The yarrow's botanical name derives its name from the legendary Greek hero Achilles who, heeding Aphrodite's counsel, employed it to treat the wounds he and his fellow Greeks, notably Telephus, sustained during the protracted siege of Troy.

Its therapeutic qualities have been recognized since ancient times, to such an extent that remnants have been discovered within a Neanderthal burial site in Iraq, dating to circa 60,000 BCE. Traditionally utilized by Native Americans and in Ayurvedic practices, yarrow also held significant importance in China, where it was employed not only for medicinal purposes but also in the divination of the I Ching. Until World War I, it was considered an unparalleled remedy for wounds and cuts.

Its affinity with the earth element is profound, to the extent that its presence not only nurtures the health of nearby vegetation but also wards off pests. Moreover, it plays a role in preventing soil erosion and draws in bees and butterflies.

It possesses a grounding energy that enables one to cultivate resilience and bravery to confront the trials of life. We can drink it as an herbal tea or use it as an amulet. Bunches of yarrow or scattered flowers on the doorstep keep away diseases and unwelcome presences, instead attracting benevolent ones, including loved ones from whom we are separated.

• THE MAGIC OF THE FLOWER •

The yarrow's medicine roots us and heals the wounds of the soul and body. It helps us to go through painful moments in a balanced way and paves the way for healing.

apple blossom

MALUS DOMESTICA

Inseparable from the vibrant energy of spring, amid the gentle hum of bees and beneath the azure canopy of the glorious season, bathed in the soft light that tenderly kisses the awakening buds, this flower speaks to us of rebirth, abundance, beauty, health, and love.

The apple blossom, renowned for its captivating fragrance, beckons pollinating insects with an irresistible allure, serving as a vital force that sustains the cycle of life upon which all nature flourishes.

The Celts used it during wedding ceremonies to bless the newlyweds and to decorate the bedrooms to foster desire. Meanwhile, in Christian tradition, the apple tree represents the very temptation that led to the fall of Adam and Eve, dooming them to a mortal existence.

The apple blossom truly acknowledges that passion has its darker facets, yet it aids in soothing these elements. It encourages us to embrace our higher selves and reveals the beauty in accepting the present moment with all its nuances.

Fertility, sensuality, temptation: presenting someone with an apple blossom is akin to pledging a vow of love and passion. Let's choose it in magical rituals for health, in love spells, and whenever we want to evoke abundance, happiness, and personal power, but also to create ceremonies of thanks toward the earth.

Its buds can be enclosed in sachets as amulets to encourage abundance, dried and burned as incense, or dissolved in liquid wax to create real love candles.

• THE MAGIC OF THE FLOWER •

The apple blossom is an invitation, a promise of the delicious fruit that will nourish and satisfy us. Herein lies its magic, reminding us to trust in a life that nourishes and loves us.

GARDEN OF THE SENSES

honesty

LUNARIA REDIVIVA

The lilac blossoms streaked with violet emit a delicate fragrance, but it is the fruits of the honesty—resembling iridescent moons or silver coins—that are unforgettable.

Native to Southern Europe, honesty is found along roadside edges, in damp and shady meadows, and beside watercourses, in keeping with its lunar nature. Its name evokes the legend that this flower grows spontaneously next to the homes of honest people.

The flowers bloom between April and May, and it is toward the end of July that the characteristic dry fruits, the silicles, appear. Typically they harbor six seeds, and when peeled, they unveil a pearly, iridescent core that evokes the image of a moon or a gleaming silver coin.

Precisely because of its appearance, honesty is still used in lunar rituals aimed at celebrating femininity and attracting prosperity and wealth. It is attributed magical powers related to fortune, and when used as a talisman, it can ward off negative energies and evil spirits.

As a member of the Brassicaceae family, honesty is not only edible but also contains nervonic acid, a compound found in breast milk. This makes it a valuable supplement for premature infants or when there is an insufficient supply of breast milk.

• THE MAGIC OF THE FLOWER •

Honesty's milky and beneficial presence, which reminds us of the magic of the moon, helps us to welcome ourselves and to be honest, transparent, and authentic.

GARDEN OF THE SENSES

baobab

ADANSONIA DIGITATA

Boasting immense and resplendent blooms of a brilliant white, the baobab stands as the largest flowering organism on planet earth.

Also called the "tree of life," the baobab can live for more than two thousand years, and within numerous African traditions, it is revered as an ancestral figure. Native to Africa and Australia, it is in fact the largest succulent in the world, with its trunk retaining a great deal of water in its fibers.

Solid, fully present, and rooted in Mother Earth, this tree embodies abundance and nurtures life, generously offering itself in every aspect. The bark is woven into baskets and nets and crafted into canoes. The leaves, roots, and seeds are not only edible but also possess healing properties; the twigs provide a refreshing quencher of thirst, and the fruit peel serves as a substitute for tobacco and as an insect deterrent. The flower is magical and extraordinary; it opens at sunset, white and majestic, and shines in the starry night, allowing itself to be pollinated by bats and nocturnal butterflies.

It is a guardian flower that invites us to embrace the shadow and shows us how the most precious things of our being are contained in it. The baobab blossom speaks the language of mystery, compelling us to sense our unity with the cosmic consciousness and its plentifulness; it extends an invitation to join the perpetual exchange of generosity and gratitude.

• THE MAGIC OF THE FLOWER •

Embodying the magic of knowing how to stay in the void to prepare the beauty of one's own flowering, the baobab teaches us the art of patient, confident, and fruitful waiting.

GARDEN OF THE SENSES

echinacea

ECHINACEA PURPUREA

Purple petals surround a spiny center, similar to a hedgehog, which the name echinacea refers to. Through its unconventional beauty, this flower speaks to us of protection and strength.

Due to its beneficial and healing properties, echinacea has been one of the sacred plants of Native Americans, who have primarily utilized it as a remedy for infectious diseases and as an antidote for rattlesnake bites. They have also traditionally smoked it and chewed its roots during the sweat lodge ritual to withstand the heat longer and thus intensify the purification process.

Renowned for its immune-boosting qualities, this plant is a formidable partner in maintaining physical health and overall well-being. It can be hung in sickrooms, burned to create purifying incense, or brewed into a tea using its leaves and roots.

When worn as an amulet or placed near the home, it is believed to draw in wealth and fertility. Carrying dried seeds and petals in one's wallet is said to lure financial prosperity, while placing them in shoes or using them in a ritual bath is thought to give the body strength and promote healing.

Echinacea can also be employed to strengthen and make any type of ritual faster and more effective, as well as intensify both our own magical and psychic energies and those of the surrounding environment.

• THE MAGIC OF THE FLOWER •

Drawing upon the body's innate ability to heal itself and the boundless generosity of the natural world, echinacea encourages us to maintain a harmonious and mutually beneficial connection between our own bodies and the earth.

mallow

MALVA SYLVESTRIS

An emblem of softness and welcome, the mallow has thin flowers of a tender violet, expressing maternal sweetness and loving delicacy.

The name derives from the Greek adjective *malkós*, which means "soft" and refers to the emollient properties conferred by the presence of a large amount of mucilage.

Horace tells us that the Romans habitually fed on it, knowing its beneficial qualities. Charlemagne, a passionate connoisseur of healing plants, imposed its cultivation in his imperial gardens. In the Middle Ages, it was used for kidney stones and biliary inflammations.

Mallow has an all-encompassing maternal care energy that softens and sweetens everything. It protects and soothes the mucous membranes and fights coughs, sore throats, and inflammations of the digestive system. Being a flower linked to women's health, it can be used in every phase of the body's transformation, even during pregnancy and breastfeeding.

It is widely acknowledged for its potent protective properties, to the extent that the leaves were traditionally interred at the entrances of stables to safeguard the livestock and their milk. When carried as an amulet or applied as an ointment, it was believed to repel evil spells.

Taken as an infusion, mallow can lead us to a state of calm and serenity, softening our edges and balancing overly hot emotions.

• THE MAGIC OF THE FLOWER •

The mallow encourages openness, flexibility, and tolerance, helping us to flow especially if we feel closed and rigid. It pushes us to trust others and to come out of loneliness.

marshmallow

ALTHAEA OFFICINALIS

With its charming and reassuring presence, standing up to six feet tall, the marshmallow thrives alongside waterways and in damp marshlands, gracing these spaces with the beauty of its delicate white or pink blossoms.

The marshmallow's botanical name comes from the Greek *althein*, which means "to heal." In mythological imagery, Althaea, the mother of Deianira and Meleager, was a controversial character. Ironically, far from being a healer, Althaea actually ended up killing her son Meleager in a fit of anger.

Inherently linked to the element of water, the marshmallow's beauty is understated but commands attention, serving as a constant reminder of its dependable presence.

Its roots, rich in mucilage, were used in fertility and aphrodisiac rituals but also to soften and protect the person in their vulnerable aspects. It is a flower that offers comfort, helping us to glide through life's events without too much resistance.

With marshmallow flowers and leaves, we can prepare an oleolite for a self-massage that protects and relaxes us. It can be burned to cleanse spaces or set upon our altar—or in a selected spot within the home—to attract benevolent energies. When enjoyed as an herbal infusion, it renders us more receptive and open while offering protection.

• THE MAGIC OF THE FLOWER •

The marshmallow's gentle nature makes it a benevolent giant, teaching us how everything is easier when we choose softness.

Bouquets

FROM THE GARDEN OF THE SENSES

If we seek softness, openness, and inner flexibility, we combine mallow and marshmallow.

To promote abundance and fertility, we choose echinacea and apple blossom.

If we want to strengthen bonds or favor new ones, we compose a bouquet with greater periwinkle and clover, or give an orchid.

Yarrow, honesty, and the precious flower of the baobab remind us to be authentic.

photographic summary

garden of the psychic

MORNING GLORY

PASSION FLOWER

BLUE LOTUS

POPPY

BOBINSANA

JASMINE

ELDERBERRY

HONEYSUCKLE

WISTERIA

IRIS

garden of the heart

ROSE

PEONY

HIBISCUS

LILY

AGAPANTHUS

AMARYLLIS

HORTENSIA

CHRYSANTHEMUM

GERANIUM

TULIP

garden of the sun

HELICHRYSUM

SUNFLOWER

ZAGARA

MAGNOLIA

ZAGARA

MAGNOLIA

FRANGIPANI

BROOM

CARNATION

EDELWEISS

ST. JOHN'S WORT

CORNFLOWER

garden of the inner child

CHAMOMILE

CALENDULA

DAISY

PRIMROSE

FORGET-ME-NOT

LILY OF THE VALLEY

VIOLA

AZALEA

CROCUS

SNOWDROP

garden of the wind

LAVENDER

NARCISSUS

QUEEN ANNE'S LACE

SOWBREAD

BUTTERCUP

MILK THISTLE

ANGELICA

ANEMONE

HEATHER

VERBENA

garden of the senses

CLOVER

ORCHID

GREATER PERIWINKLE

YARROW

APPLE BLOSSOM

HONESTY

BAOBAB

ECHINACEA

MALLOW

MARSHMALLOW

TEXT BY
Anastasia Mostacci

Anastasia Mostacci has nurtured a great interest in visible and invisible connections from an early age. Her academic pursuits included philosophy and yoga, paralleled by a dedicated exploration of the plant kingdom. She learned to identify and understand plants, derive nourishment from them, and craft remedies. Since 2015, she has been orchestrating projects and initiatives designed to enhance the dialogue between humans and nature. Accompanied by plant spirits, she leads evolutionary journeys focused on a knowledge of and relationship with the verdant world.

ILLUSTRATIONS BY
Giada Ungredda

Giada Ungredda is an Italian illustrator and graphic designer with a voracious appetite for fantasy and steampunk narratives, always envisioning fantastical realms. She has been drawing for as long as she can remember, and in her free time, she writes stories and illustrates them with watercolors, pencils, and pens. Since 2020, she has been producing botanical and educational illustrated boards for dissemination projects. Her artwork graces the pages of *Healing Animals* for Vivida.

All the photos on pages 157–159 are from Shutterstock.